The Book of Knowledge

Books by Dara Wier

Blood, Hook & Eye (1977)
The 8-Step Grapevine (1980)
All You Have in Common (1984)
The Book of Knowledge (1988)

The Book of Knowledge

poems by
Dara Wier

Carnegie Mellon University Press
Pittsburgh 1988

Acknowledgements

Thanks to the editors of magazines in which these poems first appeared: "Update on Jekyll and Hyde," *American Poetry Review;* "Homo Duplex," "Last Confession," *Balcones;* "Daytrip to Paradox," *The Black Warrior Review;* "Rolando's Fissure," *Denver Quarterly;* "Euthanasia," "Past Sorrow," *Massachusetts Review;* "The Gift," *New Virginia Review;* "Old Fashioned," *North American Review;* "Little Black Clay Angel," *Open Places;* "Lot's Wife," *Three Rivers Poetry Journal;* "Little Black Tangrams," "Nude Descending a Staircase," *Willow Springs.*

Thanks to Peter Dixon and Bonnie Miller for artwork.

I would like to thank the University of Alabama for a research grant for the summer of 1984.

Publication of this book is supported by grants from the National Endowment for the Arts in Washington, D.C., a Federal agency, and from the Pennsylvania Council on the Arts.

Library of Congress Catalog Card Number 87-71459
ISBN 0-88748-066-7
ISBN 0-88748-067-5 (Pbk.)
Copyright©1988 by Dara Wier
All rights reserved
Printed and bound in the United States of America
First Edition

Contents

Old-Fashioned / 9
Rolando's Fissure / 12
Last Confession / 14
The Teacher Said / 17
For a Book about Legendary Indian Maidens / 18
Lycanthropia / 21
Update on Jekyll and Hyde / 24
Little Black Clay Angel / 25
Euthanasia / 27
Miracle at Medzhegoria / 30
Permission / 33
Little Black Tangrams / 36
The Flood / 41
Among the Atavistic Missing What Is (Cold As)
    Two Times Two Is Four, Harsh and Pitiless / 43
Bon Ton Sur #4 / 48
Miss X on Crystal Vision / 50
Daytrip to Paradox / 54
Lot's Wife / 56
Past Sorrow / 58
Nude Descending a Staircase / 60
The Gift / 62
The Boy / 64
Theodur Sprinkles / 66
Homo Duplex / 70

And what is the fourth dimension? It is the endlessness of knowledge—

William Carlos Williams

for Michael

Old-Fashioned

Next to my best friend I woke up,
    small and deep
in the unfamiliar middle

of her parents' late night quarrel
    over faithlessness,
terrible to find her in such danger.

I wanted her whom I pictured the picture
    of happy-go-lucky to sleep.
I didn't want to turn my face to see

what hers showed or if now she knew
    or had known all along or never.
Her mother was so young, beautiful,

dark-eyed and quick; their walls, thick-
    textured and creamy like cake frosting,
were fancy and rich with filigreed frames,

watercolors of Italian bridges
    and pastels of Parisian streets.
Her father's dog was a dangerous German shepherd,

her mother's car an exotic Buick Electra
    she could take for granted.
This was the modern world I'd been denied.

Her mother wanted to know who the other woman was;
    her father didn't care.
While I listened to their familiar voices

I pictured them a foot apart, no closer
    than my friend, fat, faceless, sleeping
next to me in her bed. I pictured the dark

house shrink around us like a muscle.
    Her parents' voices rose over the pale moon
globe we'd left lit in the room for our own

late night talk of travel beyond our planet
    and the men we knew would soon walk
on the moon above us. Her parents' voices

traveled through a new atmosphere,
    one from which no words escaped.
We were on our way to somewhere unknown together

when over something I don't remember
    we parted company.
Soon her father would be gone and later

she'd grow slim and pretty as her mother,
    her mother the same
as if she were a picture.

When I went back to visit we sat together
    on the side of the same bed,
working hard to say what we'd become.

Her mother called us through the house
    for supper. Glowing in the golden light
of too many candles, Italian bridges

and Parisian streets glowed in their beautiful faces.
    When to emphasize her thought
my friend touched me on my knee

I flinched. It made me think she'd forgiven
    everything I'd understood and not forgotten.

Rolando's Fissure

When I was very young
over and over I'd picture
a woman coming across a green field of rye
in a straight, tight skirt,
taking small steps,
biting her lip,
until she'd arrive
at a low stone wall
where she'd pause before hopping
to gather her strength
and check her balance,
remembering herself
when she was a girl
about to land
home, flat-footed,
solid winner
in the chalky lines
of the hopscotch squares,
but, once over the wall,
finding herself,
her two spike heels
drilled irretrievably,
deadly down
through the eyes,
down past cerebrum
and cerebellum,
down past joy
and anger, past
pity and recollection,
along the two sides

of Rolando's fissure,
her full weight increased
in the descent of her fall,
deep in the brain
of the poor body
lain down
close to the wall
for warmth and for shade
just on the other side,
suddenly blind and struggling under her.

Last Confession

    Half-gongs and trembling
Clangs, distant bells
    From the parish church

Came to me
    In an unfamiliar bed.
And twisted sounds

    Of remote sirens
Early in the not-yet-
    Light I couldn't see

Through panels of sheer curtains
    Began clearing my head.
So I thought *Easter, it's Easter*

    Morning. Instead of rejoicing
I pushed myself back to sleep.
    I didn't want to witness

Divinity reclaiming man's body
    Forever. Mustn't have
God rejoiced when stepping into my body

    He found such a seamless garment
So fit, like nothing else,
    Like no garment at all.

To have known all at once
    The enchantment of our senses—
How passion turns tension

    Into sweetness, desire
Into being, how we eat emptiness
    Out of our bodies, how we drink

Down necessity. In the eternal
    Give and take, I can imagine
A good and curious

    God might want to be like us.
To taste cool water or take up
    The smell of a far-off fire

Or let his mouth cover the mouth
    He's known he's wanted forever.
In my warm guest bed I remembered

    A priest's voice,
Bodiless behind his purple velvet drape,
    Listening to all the sins

I didn't believe I'd committed. Still
    I did not betray my body
By calling my pleasures wrong.

    The priest had said be grateful,
It could be your last confession,
    God might call for you tomorrow.

I was thinking of the priest's mistake
    And my own will
To stop the bells and sirens

    When in the now-transparent light
My pale friend appeared just inside my door,
    His white cheek like a sick moon,

His eyes round, liquid and polished.
    He asked me to come down the hall
To look through the doorway

    Into his dim bedroom
Where his wife lay on her side, still
    In a white gown,

Loose and sheer, like the glass curtains
    I'd looked for the sun through,
Looking for all the world

    Forever dead and gone.

The Teacher Said

Imagine someone you love is dead.
Now build them the heaven you'd put them in.
Look for heaven in *Life* and *Look* and look
while you're at it for hell. For hell
is another place we'll have to build.
Find a terrible fire, hook and ladders,
red as waxed apples and dark as rich soil.
Look at the ten tiny firemen, already burnt
in their clumsy helmets and coats, someone,
someone's little sister, falling, falling
faster over the safety bars of a seven-story
landing, falling into a safety net on fire.
And find a face so forlorn as it looks on
and feels she's gone. Remember nobody's
heroic, nobody is saved, no one gets out alive.
Paste it to your posters and we'll tack it
to the board. Right next to the
U-T-FULL birds and composite flowers
you drew for your fathers and mothers.
Let's strive to keep our edges just inside
the lines. Remember to ask permission
before cutting out the picture of the corpse
preserved four thousand years in peat.
See how it shines as if a well-paid servant
lovingly rubbed it daily. Take care
when you use your scissors not to run
or climb on rickety chairs. Be obedient,
be tidy, be so careful, be very sweet.

For a Book about Legendary Indian Maidens

*who leaped from cliffs into raging torrents
when disappointed in love,
I would appreciate hearing from anyone . . .*

And who wouldn't.
Mrs. *Violet Moore* of *427 Cooley Street*,
please, of *Montezuma, Georgia*, please,

Dear Madam, Dear One, Mrs. Moore,
suicide's no amusing distraction.
If disappointment in love is what

you're after, don't ridicule
these women you speak of as maidens.
Mrs. Moore, I question your motives.

It might improve your character immeasurably
if you would volunteer for humanitarian service.
On the contrary, collecting specific,

historical evidence such as you mention
can do nothing to comfort the rest of us.
We have been disappointed in love, Mrs. Moore,

but not for long. I bet you keep
your distance from all kinds of torrents.
How many maidens does it take

to make a legend? Are you disappointed
in love? Rage? Rage is a tantrum.
Rage lives on loss. I may be all wrong.

You may be thinking of saving yourself
from a fate worse than death. Isn't failure
always a failure of courage?

Do you find the maidens courageous?
Are you disappointed with your findings?
Mrs. Moore, let's talk

about loss. The Indians lost everything.
I lost my grandmother's gold and diamond cross.
Somebody won the sweepstakes.

Somebody won the war.
The woman screaming curses down the sidewalk
lost her mind. Somebody won the lover's heart

forever. The clock loses time.
It cost the man everything but he won
custody of his children.

Mrs. Moore, I sense you have a busy mind.
I find myself wondering over your tone.
I picture your book's illustrations.

I can't get it out of my mind.
Is the death of a woman lyrical?
Is her death proof you find—

Or is she merely humorous?
A busy way to pass your busy time?
Something you'll decorate your living room with,

something you'll offer your guests,
like two dozen lemon *petit fours*
on tastefully hand-painted plates?

Lycanthropia

    Over the black and white
checkered studio couch,
        across the dew-laden

oil painting of calla lilies
      and stock-
    still glass-eyed lizards

        the furious window unit blew
its storm of coldest air,
    and over me, in my pink silk gown,

      under my satin quilt,
rose-colored and stitched
    by hand, my dark hair

was cold to touch.
    In the polished mahogany
      tabletop, in the dark

    mirror of the picture window,
my reflection, uncanny, reverted,
      was my company

each everning. Very late
      when everyone else was asleep
    I waited for Morgus

    the Magnificent
to introduce me to horror,
      to longing,

to fear in the black and white
    face of the lonely boy-wolf.
        Across the room, an inch

    out of reach beneath
the television's glass face
      his quizzical look

into my eyes worked
    against the grain
      of the single hairs

    emerging shaft by shaft
      over his delicate brow.
To what bad blood was he heir

    and by what instinct
  by what unknown agent
did he stir in me

    so much love
I wanted him
      night after night

        to reappear,
to discard his human form.
    I didn't care

if his fangs sunk deep
        into the throats
    of sleeping children,

    I didn't care
as the dull yellow petals
    of the wolfbane fell,

and the dim light fell deeper,
    and the wolf's mask
        fell over his boy's face,

    I fell away from my cold quilt
into the breathless call of invited fear
        and the loup garou's silent

twitch when his foot along his fog-
        laden path fell,
    and the terror-stricken town people's

        unbaited trap snapped, far away
from my family's sleep, beyond
    my cold heart, out of my parents' house.

Update on Jekyll and Hyde

When you live alone with no one else
what's left to do but fight with yourself?
Over sex. When you masturbate
how long does it take before you quarrel
with your style? One more mile
and you're out of control. The corral
just keeps numb animals dumb. Lucky for you
they come around for watering and feed.
A dozen roosters in the chicken pen
pecked your pair of hens to death.
You get what you expect, yes? Better
than anyone else. But on kind days
when the weather's fine and bluebirds nest
and the slag in your pond is settled
you're a good-looking neighbor nodding
to clear-eyed children bicycling by.
You've fixed bowls of crusts to give them
for them to feed your geese.
In the new stall your new foal stands
like a quick shadow nuzzling its mother.
The garden's tilled and sown and mulched.
The bank's renegotiated your loan.
The stone lions that guard your gate
practically lie down with the lambs.

Little Black Clay Angel

I have a cheap little angel
    whose cobalt clapper hides

under the fired clay folds
    of her shining black skirt,

so when I shake her shoulders
    or lift her

by her rock-hard hair
    her high notes gently

call me, always,
    always hungry,

to a table set for angels,
    a feast of abundance,

a table set for eight, eight
    others like me, all

equally hungry, all in a hurry
    to lick their sticky plates.

I see how she suffers shyly,
    she holds hurt hard,

and hoards humiliations;
    she knows it's a tug-o-war,

she homes in on hurt.
    I give her everything

that's harmed us
    and I see that she suffers,

but her hollow little body
    is a miraculous pitcher

with a built-in bottomless pit.

Euthanasia

        My mother argues
     against euthanasia,
inelegantly, between disgusts,

          over knotted hair in hairbrushes
    and Yugoslavian adolescents'
confirmed ecstatic visions.

          Across five cells of fast Fujica film
    the Mother of God is fixed.
It's hard to look

        her dead in the eye.
    With a twist across her mouth,
fasts to death are sins,

        she says, her philosophy's
    gone by the boards.
Her philosophy, her stoney church,

        turns everything into loss,
    every loss into practical necessity.
She'll save us from pecuniary embarrassment.

        She'll send the sinner,
   if necesary,
temporal calamities.

        But bliss. When
    did heaven's four rejoicing waters
last soak her through and through?

So she feels bad.
As good as she is, she finds herself
not the agent of a single miracle.

Instead she finds her heart
congenitally weak and weakening,
her husband coming up with strings

of killer illnesses,
all of her children gone
and going wrong. Who's left

to tend the garden with?
No little girls to clothe
in rings of May Day wreaths,

no little boys to clean
up and dress, no one left
to drag along to Stations of the Cross.

I loved most
her homely cotton scarves.
She smoothed them tight around my head,

the better for me
to pretend
I was old and blessed.

Sadly she touches
beneath her blouse
near her shoulder blade

       the patch of white tape
    that regulates her heart.
Her silk blouse is becoming

       on her slim frame.
  All skin and bones she is,
but her doctors don't know why.

       And angels. She says
  who sees them anymore.
Only the little band of brothers

      dedicated to their service
  and her one kooky friend
who's seen in a vision

      his angel's name is *Fred*.
  She looks across the room
for my father, buck sargeant

     in their sodality of misery.
  Throughout her argument
he's been silent as the grave.

      Pity I can't tell her
  how much I've believed in miracles,
how many times a day I've prayed.

Miracle at Medzhegoria

Between two plump japonica trees,
lush with their slippery seeds

inside their delectable, unreliable fruit,
my shining gym set gleamed silver

set in concrete, boasted its blue ladder,
green swing and red, two-seated glider.

I knew in my knees the silver second
I learned to pump my legs myself and thus

save myself having to ask.
I kicked my way into another world

where I could live alone.
I saw I could be happy

even without my father. Tonight
he sails on a hydrofoil boat

across an ancient sea to witness
a miracle-in-progress at Medzhegoria.

There's no access to apparition room
itself for the likes of him.

He pays to kneel among the faithful,
finding their way by the thousands

to keep holy vigil and hold holy candles
(when their wax drips it doesn't scorch),

to glimpse young visionaries
revealing themselves on the way

to their beds and private, deflated dreams,
pausing to translate to clerical translators

of eastern and western languages
what Our Lady of Permutations has to say

of an evening. Even when he's traveled
halfway around the world

his faith remains faith in another's belief.
I'm so happy I could die he says

and he means it. So there he goes
smelling around, picking up signals,

checking out the town where he sees
it's rare a house has running water.

The pigs in his host's front yard
are tame as friendly cats.

An old man in a tattered sweater
all day long sits in the corner

and coughs in his dirty sleeve.
On account of the miracle his daughter

makes a small living off boarders.
Especially Americans enjoy paying extra.

Their presents, soaps and sachets,
tinned hams and duck-handled umbrellas,

turn a small profit in her town.
I can see him now, his slight limp

and shortened gait, deferential,
grateful, pious, happy.

Permission

    I'd been back to visit my family.
Not to seek permission.
      Permission I'd learned

came late, came sparingly,
      from no one but myself.
  Clean-breaking waves

      along the Gulf shoreline
and bladed light the sun cast
  like precious metal

    along the edge
of every surface gave way
  to tourist traps, junk shops,

My-O-Mys and home-cooked seafood joints.
  Permission had had to wait.
    Flocks of tourists

    in raucous summer colors
lugged along their sacks of greasy lotions,
  their easy chairs,

their canvas bags and igloo coolers.
    Straying children loosened the distance
  between the busy highway

and wide blue waters.
To be named the cause
of so much sorrow

I couldn't help,
but it made me think
at whose expense—

Next to hundreds
of 1 × 1 stakes
shy Least Terns nested

in a sanctuary's designated area.
I told myself not to worry,
families can't help themselves.

It may be impossible
to believe love is not dangerous.
Impossible to see

each of us clearly
as the white stakes
hammered down

to protect the nesting terns.
As I rode on, off the coastline,
into familiar farmlands

        I saw a man fall on his lawn
on top of a woman
        who was bright red all over.

He ran after the woman
            with the big branch he carried.
    All of the others,

        the children, old men and women,
all of the others ran behind
            to see what would happen.

Or to save themselves
        from something I couldn't see.
            The woman I saw was on fire.

    The man ran after her
to beat out the flames,
            and to save her.

Little Black Tangrams

1

No one felt in the dark for his hat.
No one budged an inch.
Thus the story draws to its end.
No one felt over the edge
of her silk pocket to touch her parking ticket.
No one even wished to
walk out of the dark to the street.

2

Over the transparent page I traced my name.
I thought about The Bird That Turns Around,
How To Blow A Brick Over, What To Do
While Waiting For The Doctor, Answers To
Problems On Page 2,000, The Chair That
Comes To You, The Mysterious Paper Purse,
The Universe Around Us, *Lift To Erase.*

3

Those days everything I thought trembled
through the rotating blades of an electric fan.
The way my voice moved through it.
The way my fingers shook.
I wore a two-tiered hat.
A dead mule is huge.
The man with the stick was fat.

4

A dead deer has the face of a rat.
Last night I watched seven white deer
walk single file across the black edge,
the levee's border.
Slowly, each one looked me over,
saw I was sleeping, and soon came closer
to lick my face all over.

5

All fall I played at being a slave.
In the red embers of fires I made
I burned slips of paper with politicians' names
to pass the time.
I cooked rich soups of dragonflies.
I learned to aim an arrow
through a devilhorse's brain.

6

I sat alone by the water.
They trusted me with the river.
When United Fruit Company boats
headed for port, upriver,
I called out to sailors,
down came stalks of bananas
to snag and bring up to the batture.

7

When the polls opened until the polls closed
two men dangled their rifles over their shoulders
and pretended they couldn't be seen.
The men and women who came were embarrassed.
They looked down at the white glare
of crushed shells at their feet.
They looked off into the distance.

8

In the hot sun on the wooden platform
I stood waiting for the icehouse doors to open.
I wanted to be asked inside
the cool bricks of smoking water, frozen
and squared in fifty-pound blocks,
rattling along belts of silver rollers.
I wanted to be cool and dry.

9

The women were left locked in the house.
The rifle's blue-black barrel shone
in the corner against the white, white wall.
Somewhere in the swamps around us
a man threw himself against the dark.
I couldn't understand why our lights were on.
I wondered if he would drown.

10

I was afraid of the iridescent algae pool,
hit with glaze after an afternoon storm,
lifted like a giant keyhole,
lit by the great green eyeball behind it,
watching me, watching me turn away,
watching me look back, watching me, for all I knew,
catch my breath, not wanting to give it back.

11

We walked into the parking lot
after 10 o'clock mass on Sunday.
A car's blur crossed our path
so close I felt the heat of the sun
in the hot wind off its fender.
They only meant to scare us.
I felt then what my prayers might have been.

12

That afternoon someone decided to slaughter the
                                                         rabbits.
They held the scruffs of their necks,
whacked their soft brown crowns
with cracked baseball bats.
Each one bled through the nose.
We fed their guts to the alligator
by the shed in the deep, deep hole.

13

I watched them kissing, kissing in sorrow,
in the sitting rooms in the funeral parlor.
They were drinking *cafe au lait*
and eating ham sandwiches.
Yes, there were so many flowers.
I didn't want to be kissed in sorrow.
I didn't want to be patted or pitied.

14

The squeak and thump and mist of flit
as someone pumped sprays of insecticide.
It fell over my face, like a blessing,
like a tingling sensation in my fingers,
like a thousand evaporating lessons,
it fell on the oil lamp's wick.
The flame danced. It wobbled, dipped and brightened.

The Flood

The obese man with a goiter,
it looked so tender,
sloshed a bucket of dirty water
over my windshield's streaks of dust
and dead insects. He had tires
to sell me and oil and air
and for half a dollar
he'd unlock his cellar
where he kept his spectacular
two-headed calf.

By his way of asking he wanted to know
why I was passing through Rush,
and where, if I could remember, was there.
He motioned me over, took my money,
pointed where the river turned nearer,
added I shouldn't worry,
odds were good against another disaster.
How was I to explain to a stranger
how deep in love I was, and stunned.

Up the road the flood had set dead deer
to rot up high in trees. Cedars, elms
and sycamores, all the scraggly bushes
and tall grasses leaned hard in one direction.
Every broken post and twisted guardrail
descended down its gully.
Over the clean new sand of a roadside park

I stopped and watched two lovers
open the green wings of their car doors
to let their sweet music drift down
to the fish in the river and up
to the quarter moon.

Two nights before they'd have been underwater.
They'd have lost one another.
There'd have been no time to wave goodbye.
Maybe she'd have seen his eyes
through the instant flash
as they fell apart, almost bowing
to one another in the last, liquid notes
of a slow, sexy dance.
Maybe he gave her his last breath
of air when he kissed her. Maybe
he held a loose swatch of her billowing sleeve.

So she seemed to struggle, but didn't,
but couldn't be still any longer.
Maybe she knew this would happen.
Maybe he wanted it to.
Today they're safe from danger.
Their kisses come and go
and when they breathe they take time
to breathe one another's air.
They hold one another as though their bodies
fold the seam of a spectacular current,
and lean hard into one another
like headwaters joining a flood.

Among the Atavistic Missing What Is (Cold As) Two Times Two Is Four, Harsh and Pitiless

Her parents looked like two sides
of the same girl's face.

A girl of situations,
she insisted she was adopted.

She pictured herself
on cartons of milk.

And who was I—to let on
I didn't believe her—

mistrust had the next
to cruellest touch.

I threw a sack of salt
over my shoulder.

I loved her like a sister.
I believed my bratty neighbor

the summer he taught me
sun-warmed tar we pulled

from the seams of roads
whitened my teeth

so they gleamed
like a wolf's teeth,

43

gluttonous for something
delicious.

I believed my real and frightened mother
when she insisted

you're killing your father.
Who could deny it—

brothers and sisters,
everyone got older

at someone's expense.
I believe the boy

the wolf tracked
tracked something too,

a foraging bird
he was hungry to eat.

So many footprints
across so many fields

of snow, flawless worlds
of white, white asphalt,

never asking whose fault,
never fond of blame,

never keeping track.
I bet it was that lucky bird

I'd thrown expensive salt at.
Still the bird flew away home.

So the boy and I fret together
beyond the safety of meadows,

roam the wood's white wilderness,
through the mind, through the senses,

against the advice of elders,
before the fears that haunt them,

before what follows
without end.

Hard work? Do you think
it's bad luck's best joke?

Like jokes among friends
when their friendships end.

Sometimes I know how to pretend
I've been adopted by my parents.

Wasn't La Rochefoucauld funny?
As if passions had manners,

as if it all boiled down
to standards.

The saying goes
things belong

to those who want them
most. Most of all

we want to know
whose dust it is

we're eating. Cheaters?
It's funny to think

someone might care
to put the world's eyeglasses

on the ground face down.
A long, cold stare round

about now brings me closer
to surrender. If I'm lucky

I'll stumble
upon 15th century illustrations

of men devoted to compassion.
I should make it a practice

to collect nervous rats
in my attic to gnaw

at my knots of ignorance.
That girl did have sickly parents

and an unmarried sister
who wasn't pretty

and her mother cooked plain spaghetti
while her father polished his chrome.

I used to like to visit their home
and listen to her list

the dresses, rings and flowers
she intended to be given for gifts.

I liked to look at sheer flounces,
dust ruffles and ceremonial valences,

and the rose-covered curtains
that covered their roses.

With equanimity, composure, sang-froid,
serenity, benevolence, equity,

sympathy, believe me, *trust me* is the joke
that thought who broke whose heart.

Bon Ton Sur #4

It's a happy haircut,
one you eat,

but don't get
on the white blazing countertop

in the click
of fat chopsticks, in the drip

of whatnots, when
it passes the plate

as it passes the buck,
it's the manufactured hen's tooth

and shoots
in the dark

in the quick
liquid eyes of nude mice,

two donkeys cooperating to climb,
bred and bred down,

a hundred little ladders
too tiny to climb,

it's calling the dog
who's out too late

in a soupy fog,
what are friends for,

it dresses in splinters,
what's so wrong,

it bounces along,
falls off a log

to see which side
bread's buttered on

round the little cultured highway's
gentle subtle bend

Masterpieces Reasonable
the greedy sign said.

Miss X on Crystal Vision

consciousness

New sleep was the new babe in town.

sensation

Sleek as spit on thawing ice
over the hillside of thawing snow.

perception

Now that I've been there I know how it goes.
Though not so, you know, so-so.
Sleep sloshed around in my skull, it foamed.

space

Inside deep in the infinite middle inside
the crystal ball I'd been set down
in the lobby over the logo
of the crowded Nouveau Deco Cultural Hall.

emotion

Some kind of wishy-washy music waited to begin.
The house lights blinked and blinked again.
Up the sleep of the easy slope,
the controlled faint, fainting,
the after-image of a sudden fall,

knowledge

thought that comes in a vortex, oily,
like cold vodka pouring over expensive glass, the present
ejected out of the past, past one long flight
of black marble steps, no past at all, not after
the fall, not past the solid floor my head
would not sink into or through.

morality

The blank stare around the stranger's mouth,
can you hear me, can you feel my hand,
Miss X stared while I rushed too far too fast.
I was the wind over her face her fingers made
when she fanned the diamonds, clubs, hearts,
spades it was her turn to shuffle. I had to wait
for time and space to haggle me back again.

morality

Hair-triggered, barely there, slightly
like flash-light catches a few kinked blades of grass,
against the edge of a dampened foot's shoe leather,
that corner of plank walk rotting for weather,
the trough pressed in the grass the snake hisses through,
scattered leaves of cypress, pecan, persimmon, the shank
end of the fig's trunk, up the brink again into pieces.

knowledge

Everything's changed, nothing's name is the same,
not the meticulously restored historical monuments nor
the isolated mathematical exchanges of dollars for goods
and services, not the even-handed faith the future
stakes its life against, not the unfamiliar old words,
not the relieved face Miss X takes with her when she
                                                    goes

emotion

back through the hole she left in the crowd,
back with her thumb hitched under her shoulder strap,
through the cracks the musician makes
between each number, number than anesthesized skin,
I'm up in my numbered seat, listening.

space

Outside shallow gutters fill with silver waters
of streetlit rain fall, 10,000 splinters of electric
light take back the deep, dark distance, take up the new
post-modern skyscrapers and their Space Available
                                                    signs.

perception

I see I fell *into* to get to you, through
and through, so soaked to the bone,
I floated in holy ground.

sensation

Timid, short of letting you go,
I take it all in this gentled stride.

consciousness

Love was the first breath I took.

Daytrip to Paradox

    Just as you'd expect
my preparations were painstaking
      and exact. I took two

butane lighters and a cooler
    of ice. I knew the route
had been so well-traveled

      there'd be a store for necessities
and tobacco and liquor and axes.
   And near the Utopian village of Nucla

     three Golden Eagles watched me
from a salt cedar tree. One of them
   held its third talon hard in the eye

of a white Northern Hare. Audubon
   couldn't have pictured it better.
      Everything was perfect. Naturally

    it made me think of Siberia,
the bright inspirational star
      that's handed down the generations,

and the long, terrible nights
    of the pioneers' journey to paradise.
    The valley on the way to Paradox

    was flat, there would be no choice,
nothing to get me lost.
        Cattleguards, gates and fencing

bordered the open range. Of course
   I crossed a narrow bridge
      to get into Paradox proper.

   In the store that doubled
as town hall and post office
      there was an account book for everybody

laid square on the counter.
   No one was expected to pay
      hard cold cash in Paradox apparently.

Lot's Wife

I'm not Lot's wife
        but I think to be
a block of salt

under the best circumstances
        might be luxurious,
as close to blissful peace as possible.

Think of the smooth indentations
        a tongue works in its persistence,
simple shapes of simple wonder

that fit purpose to use.
        The smooth block of salt
in the dark shade near a hot pasture

is welcoming and serene.
        Grazing deer move toward it
as if their hooves give off perpetual

mist. Hot ice might be rising
        from each precious footstep.
Lot's wife might be nothing

but a sentimental fool,
        salt her storehouse of sorrow.
She bothers the past

and worries sinners
    who believe evil
can be gotten by and ignored.

Poor Lot's wife serves well
    her sorry purpose.
To help me remember

I'll wear two worn charms on my necklace,
    a block of hot ice
and a pillar of salt.

Religious language clothes itself
    in whatever poor symbols
our lives will afford.

Past Sorrow

In the pool along the walk
    the blind girl takes
an angry grackle shakes his head

    in and out of the water.
At first he seems angry
    because he is wet all over

but he puts his head under
    again and again. He seems so
angry he doesn't see me.

    And I have my sheet
to finish folding. It's the white sheet
    of sorrow I hold between us.

I admit it can blind us
    so our fingers smart
and grow sensitive as the practiced

    fingers of the young girl
blind since birth. I've watched her
    piece her life together

as she walks up the hill
    before my house. She doesn't see
the sorrow lining up

    along the porch railings as she passes.
She has troubles of her own.
    I once saw her slip

in her blue satin pumps and turn
    her head the way I might
to see who saw me fall.

    My sorrow is clean and ready
to put away in the cupboard.
    I know where I'll keep it

at hand if I need it,
    to unfold, to shake out,
to sleep on it.

    It takes all of my fingers
to take hold
    of this sorrow.

It takes my arms
    to shape such an embrace.
As I begin to fold the sheet

    we step closer and closer
to one another. I fold it
    and fold it

until we are face to face.

Nude Descending a Staircase

We're made to
    exclude and be
        excluded. How much

    the cubists make
        that plain
presenting their plans

        for our omniscience,
our science of the everything-all-
    at-once.

        So this is why
    innocence isn't bliss
and even

    isn't ignorance even
but a kind
    of slight

insult—cold, delicious
    soup served up
        with silver forks

    on a wet, freezing evening.
        Though we remain
permeable,

            not skintight,
not shutdown
        and not set in stone.

        Our eternal shopping lists
                flap on
the breezy line, long

and thick, dirty with data,
        lists of demographics
                full

        of the telephone ringing,
                out of time
like a baby crying,

                calming, calm
then startled
        into more cries

that can't be calmed
        by smooth talk
                or sweet song

        or the body's
                longing answer,
come here to me, come here.

The Gift

I had been thinking of Marcel Duchamp
    and the book he gave his sister.
He'd tied Euclidean geometry

    to a string to let
the four seasons and all the time
    of day and night

work it over, test it,
    offer it back to the birds
or whatever in nature would have it.

    It was his idea
to bring ideas down to earth again.
    I had been thinking

of the birth of our baby
    as she slept through the afternoon
in the solid quiet after a thunderstorm.

    I looked up
at the quiver of flowers
    in the middle of the table

and thought at first it must be me
    shaking from cold
or shaking with fears

    I wish her never tested.
Then I heard the Southern Crescent
    rattling north two blocks away

and thought of my long ride on it
    through mid-Atlantic snow
into Southern sleet and rain

to put behind me my grandfather's death
    and saw the train was the reason
the flowers were shaking.

The Boy

Across Montague Road the old man,
    my old man, my neighbor stranger,

stands so still,
    still as he, as he can,

for so long,
    so long do I watch him standing,

I think he might be dreaming,
    and if he is sleeping,

he is a young boy,
    back then he was when,

pretending as hard,
    as hard then easy it was,

as he is able,
    he was willing and able,

he stands so still,
    as he will,

no one can see him so,
    so he thinks,

he stands long like an old man,
    it's his time alone,

who sees it all,
    all there is he sees it,

as the cup of his hand,
    my hand hot around the ice cold cup,

closes around a green branch,
    idly snapped from the skinny trunk,

the way my hand closes,
    and knows it does,

around the hand my daughter,
    doubting where she goes,

gives me when she wants me,
    when it's me she wants,

to stay close,
    and he holds on,

hung over a deep cliff,
    where a tree digs in and grows,

sensing the moment,
    he knows,

the way a little petal
    flutters and falls he'll let go.

Theodur Sprinkles

        After my daughter takes her medicine
she trembles. The medicine works.
    My heart's a knot.
        Down through the flight

of bare board steps
        her frightened voice calls out
    I'm going to die,
but I know she's not.

    But her small hands shake
        and she can't walk
like a happy, happy goat.
    But I know she's getting better.

        Through her restless night
she wrestles, fighting
    her difficult breath,
        fighting up the steps.

So hard is her question,
    she fixes me with her look,
        she doesn't bother asking it.
She cries out over and over

    I've lost something. I've lost something.
    Hold me.
The long fine print of her drug's side effects
    doesn't say what it is she's lost.

      But I know she needs to sleep.
   So I don't go up.
I go outside to accuse
      the cool New England moon.

I watch my breath condense,
      float, fall and disappear.
   I think of stars I can't see
through the dim seaboard's glow.

   And the ones I can, orderly and clear,
cross-stitched inside the dark sky's skull.
      I wager everything against
   the chance one of them might fall.

      In a small plane's steady, red,
blinking signal I forget myself.
     It cuts across the jagged horizon
      beyond the tree line over town

as it heads to land near the banks
      of the Connecticut River.
   Salmon I didn't know were gone
they've said are coming back again.

   It's somebody's job to catch them.
It's somebody's job to count them all.
     Somebody's job to put them to sleep,
   to collect their thousands of eggs apiece.

      So the fish can dream they've spawned.
Somebody helps them along.
   Someone collects their glistening eggs,
      more than the visible stars,

each yolk sac, a transparent golden ball,
     like hope itself, to see
   the long future through.
Up through the hemlocks and brush

   the hatchery's lights flicker
     through the night.
The salmon eggs' new black eyes float
   in their golden amber light.

     When I lose sight
of the plane's steady signal
I turn to go inside,
    back up the steps,

past the leaves blown across the yard,
   but stop to see before me
     through the darkness of my lawn
the huge white face of a lone red hereford,

   dark holes where its eyes
look at me with wonder,
    before me in the air,
   its broad skull luminous

       before it moves
its sturdy, heavy hooves
    and shows itself
         corporeal and snorting.

Homo Duplex

        No one should be alone,
not on a night like this,
                all dressed up

to go out dreaming.
    After all it is the season.
        Yesterday morning Evening

          Grosbeaks *chee-ipped* and squawked,
around and around, bobbed
              and dipped, after seeds

on my tilted, spinning feeder.
    Pretty birds, with strong heads,
       strong beaks and striking

    yellow masks, they raid in flocks
and don't stay long.
             Not too long

ago I thought, without thinking twice,
   I thought, content
      with the eternal current

     across water's swirling circles.
I thought less
        of the underwater world

once upon a time. Unmasked, unselfconsciously
   as migrating birds, I was content to glide
      along watery halls, wide as continental

>   corridors of sky, wider than deep
> waters sleeping
>   fish call home.
>
> By chance, sometime ago I learned
>   the regular thump
>   of a treadle, working against clay
>
>   two thousand years before,
> can be replayed, restored
>   by scientists
>
> with laser needles. I remembered
>   the palm-size pot shard
>   old friends sent my son,
>
>   music to my ears, for luck,
> and how late at night—a time
>   like this,
>
> when I'm awake, and not alone,
>   nursing the baby back to sleep
>   I lean into the room, rocking
>
>   through figures woven into a rug,
> crazy dog leaping for love of its legs,
>   more legs
>
> on the funny body of the laughing lizard,
>   and fingers on the man for his bird
>   to light upon.

    Far into their world, away
from broken thought bobbing
                      up and up

beyond my ability to fix,
    or to catch in it the promise sung
        in ancient song, I look up to see

        on a broken water pot, fixed in clay,
the fraction of a lightning stroke
                      over my open door.